Graduate's Guide to Success

Graduate's Guide to Success

William J. Krutza

BAKER BOOK HOUSE
Grand Rapids, Michigan

ISBN: 0-8010-5374-9
Printed in the United States of America

Sixth printing, March 1984

WHICH WAY WILL YOU GO from here? There are all kinds of possibilities. You've probably driven to some familiar place. In most instances, you can take several different roads to get there. The shortest route. The longest way home. The most scenic route. The roundabout way when you are in no particular hurry. The way your parents go.

You have to make up your mind which way you'll go. And it all depends on your purpose.

Have you ever come across some slowpoke driver who doesn't seem to know where he is or where he is going? He looks at every gasoline station with an intense longing for directions . . . but doesn't turn in. He's the kind of fellow who is suspicious of all those "go down to the third red light, turn left, go five short blocks—count them on the right side only, turn left to a short cutoff before the curve, then go one block." Confusing instructions. No wonder many people don't like to stop and ask. Would you?

We all remember the standard joke about the fellow giving directions. Pointing down the street, and so on. He finally concludes, "You can't get there from here!" You almost believe him.

Of course, some routes follow one-way streets and highways. To go against traffic leads to catastrophe. In fact, those big red and white "wrong way" signs pop up before you if you make the mistake and go against traffic. You might even meet up with the man with the flashing red lights atop his car. You know who! And ouch!

Going down life's highway is before you. Sometimes it appears to be easy. Some people in school have given you that impression. And if you've already set some goals for yourself, you're sure to find some killjoy who'll try to tell you you can't get there from here. Besides, who wants goals so early in life, anyway?

Once in a while you'll discover you've been going the wrong way. Sometimes it'll be soon enough to make a correction before you encounter a catastrophe. Sometimes someone else will be smart enough to flash a red light—warn you that you've made a mistake.

But sometimes you'll be left all to yourself. You know you have set some definite goals: more education . . . marriage . . . a good job . . . service to others . . . special enjoyments. Since you can travel many ways, you have to make wise decisions. They were thrust on you even before you graduated. No one can make the decisions for you. You know it isn't a life or death matter to choose to go one way instead of another. The goal is ahead. Maybe you've already taken the shortest way. Maybe it doesn't matter how long it takes to arrive at your destination. But the choice is yours.

One of the complicating factors comes when

someone says to you, "Go this way." Or another tells you, "Not that way, this one." You hear all kinds of voices calling for your allegiance. Giving directions. Having plans for your future. Which voice should you listen to? Whom should you follow? What about that still small voice within?

Ah! Probably the most assuring words of direction are found in the Bible. The most proven way is to go God's way. Isaiah 30:21 proclaims, "This is the way, walk in it." Not bad advice for one just starting out on life's great journey.

When it comes to getting aligned with God, here's what Jesus said about going the right direction: "I am the way, the truth, and the life. No man comes unto the Father but through me." That's a proven one-way street. Walk down it with Jesus for the best directions.

The Lord gives us some warnings about those who try alternate routes. They might look okay. The pavement might look the same. Scenery appealing. No apparent dangers. But a wise man once declared (Prov. 14:12), "There is a way which seems right to a man, but its end is the way of death." That's just the opposite of what Christ offers if you follow His way. He offers life!

Maybe some of your friends will laugh when you turn into Christ's one-way street. They'll think it's too narrow. They want to have what they call fun. They've worked out all the appealing directions to what they conclude will be a happy life. Yep. Jesus said, "Broad is the way that leads to destruction. But narrow is the way that leads to life. Few there be who find it."

If you've found Christ's one way to happy living, consider yourself fortunate indeed. You are traveling the road that leads to life—real life! Stick to it. It's the world's only one-way street to a better life.

YOU'LL SEE ONLY ONE exception to this sign. Watch for it on the interstates. Emergency vehicles allowed to cross the median strip and head back in the other direction. You'll encounter this sign in many busy metropolitan districts —right where a 180° turn would cause confusion and traffic tie-ups.

Some states and cities have No U turn laws even though signs aren't posted. In some cases, U turns are strictly prohibited. Others allow U turns in the middle of a block but never at intersections. Some allow U turns at red lights—usually on the green arrow. You'd better know the laws before you decide to make a quick-go-back-to-where-you-came-from.

Life is sort of a busy business district or a fast traveled interstate. As a TV commercial once put it, "You only go around once." You are forced into the ever present present. You face into the future. You can't turn around and live yesterday over. You've graduated from the past. And though school days were exciting and enjoyable, you just can't turn back. Life is ahead!

Life also has an eternal, unchangeable No U turn law. It's impossible to go back to where you were a year ago, a week ago, or even an hour ago. You can't relive any situation that is past. Every moment presents new factors with which you must cope. You come past each moment only once. You can't change one moment of the past. There's no turning back. No person is ever given some special type of emergency privileges. To attempt a U turn could lead to drastic consequences. Some people who make mental U turns end up visiting head shrinks.

One famous U turn is recorded rather early in the Bible. Lot and his family were warned to get out of the wicked city of Sodom. In a hurry, you guys! They almost exceeded the speed limit in their exodus—except for Lot's wife. It says in Genesis 19:26 that she stayed behind her husband. Suddenly, because her heart was still in Sodom, she made a U turn. You know the rest of the story. "She became a pillar of salt." The U turn wasn't worth the risk involved. She couldn't live her yesterdays over again.

Jesus said this about a fellow who wanted to make a U turn: "No one who puts his hand to the plow and looks back is fit for the kingdom of God" (Luke 9:62). He impressed this on His hearers. Commitment to Jesus means keeping one's back to the past and his face set toward the future. You've graduated!

A good way to avoid any need for U turns in life is to "commit your way unto the Lord, trust also in him and he shall bring it to pass" (Ps. 37:5). With that resolve, the necessity for U turns is eliminated. It's exciting to go straight forward into the future. In that attitude one doesn't have continual regrets that desire a reliving of the past.

Since U turns are actually impossible in life, one can only commit the past to the mercy and grace of God. And in a marvelous way He takes care of it all. Besides, He wants you to go straight ahead. There's a great big life out there!

GETTING INTO EXPRESSWAY traffic at a rush hour scares many drivers. Specially beginners. In fact, some people dread this more than anything else about expressway driving. Give them the good old side streets.

You read the rules of the road booklets in drivers' ed. Remember this advice: check the flow of the inner lane of traffic as you drive on the entrance ramp. Gain speed to match that of the main flow. Merge behind the next possible vehicle. According to the booklet this is supposed to work every time.

All of us know the rule book presents the ideal situation. It pictures everyone in the mainstream driving at the stated recommended space behind the car ahead. It assumes that all drivers gladly give up their right-of-way.

Unfortunately you rarely find the ideal merging setting. Everyone seems to tailgate—specially at the rush hours. Drivers want to keep you from merging ahead of them. Behind, okay, but not ahead. They want to get home as quickly as possible. Why let you in?

Yet, if you are going to get to your destination, you have to merge. You have to get into the stream of traffic and keep going no matter how awkwardly you enter. Regardless of risks, you merge!

While you've been in school, you haven't paid much attention as to how you'd merge into the mainstream of life. When you thought of it, it was academic. Now you are faced with reality. It's a little scary. Everyone in the mainstream is bent on getting himself ahead. He doesn't want you to enter before him . . . to take his place. He'll do his best to keep you out if necessary. He doesn't care much how you enter. This is an every-man-for-himself world. What you learned in school gave you techniques, but now you have to put it into practice. It's time to merge!

Life makes the same demands of everyone. You can't avoid the mainstream if you intend to arrive at any designated goals. Life doesn't allow alternate routes that have no merging situations. Sooner or later you must merge into life as it is, not as you'd like it to be. What you've learned from books has to be tested in a dog-eat-dog world. That's just the way it is. So don't stop on the ramp.

Life calls us to face a lot of mergings. All kinds of issues travel along. We don't make an ideal merging every time. But try we must. God wants us in the mainstream. He created us for that. He doesn't want us parked along the edge watching everyone else face the ugly issues. He doesn't map out side roads that never involve us with the tough living among unfriendly people in this world. He doesn't tell us to get a lot more training.

Maybe a couple lessons from the Master will help us merge more smoothly . . . and more effectively as one of His representatives.

Remember the time Jesus was invited to a wedding. He merged right in—even producing the feast's best wine (John 2:1-11). Remember the starving crowd. He merged right in—took what was available and satisfied the entire group of five thousand (John 6:4-13). Remember the man born blind—Jesus instructed him to go wash in the pool of Siloam (John 9:1-40).

God calls every one of us to merge into the traffic of the needs of mankind. Some are starving. Some don't know what answer to give to questions such as abortion. Some have difficulties driving an honest business deal. Some are speeding to a nowhere end. There are unlimited access places for graduates to enter our needy world.

You can represent Jesus Christ as you merge into the main traffic around you. Not by a bumper sticker, but by a life. The expressway of life is filled with people with needs. Take your merging instructions from the Master and "let your light so shine before men, that they may see your good works and give glory to your Father who is in heaven" (Matt. 5:16).

Take the risk, make the entry. Graduation time opens the way for you to merge into the lives of others. God wants you to represent Him in the mainstream. But watch your fenders . . . some earthlings don't really want you there. But get in—there's room for more of your kind . . . specially for those whose goals include helping alleviate human needs.

ANY OPEN ROAD DRIVER becomes accustomed to interstate and US highway bypasses. They save considerable time when you are traveling cross-country.

A bypass simply takes us around congested city areas. We continue at the same speed and relax on our way. Since we have no particular business in the city, why be forced to pass through it as we did in the past?

Some of our parents remember the "good old days." All highways were deliberately routed through the center of our towns and cities. Highways were the means of getting from one town to the next and went through the downtown areas. Often we crept home as a weekend came to a close. Stop-and-go traffic added extra hours to all journeys. It's with joy that we now accept bypasses as one of the biggest improvements since gravel roads.

You'll soon discover some bypasses in life are most desirable. You've already learned to avoid some situations—specially evil ones. The wise Proverb collector Solomon said, "Do not enter the path of the wicked, and do not walk in the way of evil men. Avoid it; do not go on it; turn away from it and pass on" (Prov. 4:14, 15). Not bad advice for someone who is launching into life. Also not a bad way to treat evil!

Some young people seem to believe they have to head right into evil to test their strength to overcome it. Like smoking marijuana to know what it'll do to your brain . . . or drinking whiskey . . . or indulging in sex. When they experiment they believe they are experts. It's like going right into a traffic jam to prove you know how to drive. Or speeding at 100 mph. Totally unnecessary. You can prove you know how to drive at 38 mph . . . on a not-so-busy street. You can prove you're grown up by bypassing harmful indulgences better than by indulging. Try it.

Paul talks about another bypass that is most welcome and profitable in the Christian life. It's a second cousin to Solomon's advice about bypassing evil. Paul instructed Timothy to "avoid godless chatter, for it will lead people into more and more ungodliness, and their talk will eat its way like gangrene" (II Tim. 2:16, 17).

Godless talk, or talk about evil practices . . . or the entertaining of evil thoughts . . . or using four-letter words—all these can be harmful to the individual. So why not take the Christain bypass? Avoid evil chatter. Fill your mind with worthwhile words—words that build your character.

To Titus, Paul gave instruction about taking yet another bypass. He adds a new dimension to a Christian's speech. He tells the young man to take a bypass around evil talk about others. "Speak evil of no one. Avoid quarreling." Heated debate with others does neither party one bit of good. "Be gentle, and show courtesy toward all men" (Titus 3:2). It's possibly contrary to the exuberance of youth, but it sure pays off.

If one doesn't take such useful bypasses, sooner or later his life gets bogged down. It can even come to a standstill. Bypasses are for our use. Learn to use them early in life.

THE BIG ORANGE SIGNS tell us several things. Slow down. Men working. The highway is being improved. You will be temporarily inconvenienced. Detour.

All along the highway we come across these improvement signs. A gang of men. Big machinery. The smell of asphalt paving. Air hammers cracking concrete. Barricades. In some cases, big signs tell us how many state and federal dollars are being spent for the improvement (a less painful way of telling us why we pay taxes?).

Such construction signs indicate a need for repairs. Others tell us repairs or improvements are being made. The areas have deteriorated or become inadequate for present traffic.

In a few states, highway departments post a sign at the end of each construction area: "Thank you for your patience." They understand how annoying such traffic slowdowns can become.

Yet, without apology, they continue to do their work. Such construction areas are a necessary part of our country's thousands of miles of good highways. They eventually make such roads safer and more pleasant to travel.

A road without any construction areas would be one of the world's wonders. All roads deteriorate. All roads can be made safer. All roads can be reconstructed to make our trips more enjoyable. A road never needing new construction is rarer than freezing temperatures in the equatorial tropics.

Your life ahead will have its necessary construction areas. Sooner or later every graduate discovers he hasn't reached perfection. People deteriorate mentally, physically, and spiritually if they never slow down to have some reconstruction done. Such reconstruction takes planning and considerable effort. It's like going to school all over again.

But rather than doing all the work ourselves, why not turn our lives over to the constructor of the universe—Jesus Christ? He proclaimed, "Behold I make all things new" (Rev. 21:5). That concerns the ages and worlds to come. It can also be related to the day by day process of making us over again.

You probably think your school days were like a big construction job anyway. You're glad they are over for a while. But there's a good reason for construction times. God brings us into them so we might "be conformed to the image of his Son" (Rom. 8:29). And as one translator stated (II Cor. 5:17), "If any one is in Christ, he is in the process of becoming a new creation. As the old things pass away, all things become new." Schooling never ends. God isn't through with you yet.

Allow God to do the constructing necessary to make your life all He desires it to be. It'll be an improvement no matter how you look at it. He's the Master Constructor. And making us into the likeness of Jesus Christ doesn't sound bad.

THE ILLINOIS TOLLWAY COMMISSION recently made two decisions. The first pleased most motorists. The commission reduced the toll rates because it was collecting tolls faster than the law allowed the commission to pay off its bonds. What was the second action of the commission? Use the money to build more tollways . . . to collect more tolls . . . to pay off more bonds . . . to build more tollways. . . .

Some states boast they have no tollways. You pay no more than the taxes added to the gasoline prices. You ride free, so they proclaim.

Not all interstate highways are freeways, to the surprise of many. Have you ever been driving along and suddenly a tollway sign pops up. Soon you are facing a tollgate. What a surprise. Like other drivers, you pull out the needed money, drop it into the meter, and hardly wait for the green light to go on before you accelerate. It's all a part of the high cost of getting from here to there.

Many times the tollway is the fastest way home. One is willing to pay the price if he can arrive at his destination earlier and with less frustration.

Not too long after you get into life's mainstream, you'll discover nobody gets on for long on a free ride without responsibilities or consequences or expenses. This is specially true if we abuse our bodies.

Take smoking and drinking. The ads tell you all about the pleasures. But they never tell you there's a toll to pay ahead. Fact is, you pay a toll far in excess of the enjoyments offered. Possible lung cancer, emphysema, cirrhosis of the liver, heart attacks, shortened life. All these are tolls charged later on . . . to be paid somewhere down the road. And if you've seemingly escaped the tollgates now, don't consider yourself too lucky. Luck runs out. There's another pay station ahead . . . possibly when you make the final exit. It can be an "enjoy now, pay later" plan. Are you willing to pay the toll?

Moses told the early Israelis they had to live according to the law or else pay a heavy toll. In Numbers 32:23, he warned, "Be sure your sin will find you out." It didn't matter how young or old the person was. It never does. This rule is the same for all.

Paul put it another way. But the meaning is the same. "Do not be deceived; God is not mocked, for whatever a man sows, that will he also reap" (Gal. 6:7).

Whatever the activity—good or bad—we indulge in, whatever the attitude we have toward harmful personal practices (whether we sense we are paying a price or going scot-free), we'll pay the tolls. It doesn't matter whether we like the tollgate or not. Or even if we avoid the toll law by rushing through.

How much better to exercise self-control while you are still young. To enjoy life even by denying yourself indulgences in harmful substances or activities. Do that now, live happily later.

Pay toll ahead—either in sorrow, misery, pain, or death—or by those acts and attitudes that keep you healthy and free. The toll charge is in your hands.

THIS ONE SIGN BRINGS MASSES of moving steel to a grinding halt. STOP. There's a finality to the octagonal red sign's message. It means exactly what it says. And when some drivers misinterpret its message, they invite crumbled fenders, broken glass, injuries, death . . . or a policeman's written communication!

STOP doesn't mean come up to an intersection at a slow pace, look both ways, and proceed with caution. Without uttering a sound, the sign screams into our cranial capacities—STOP. Come to a complete halt. Cease moving forward. Hold it!

You are traveling along a paved country road. You come to a seemingly insignificant gravel road intersection. STOP. You mumble something about having to stop. But the red sign gives you an exact command. You stop. A quick look. Acceleration. Gravel flies.

A busy four-lane street intersects with a two-laner. Red octagonal sign. Step on brakes. Proceed after someone takes right of way. You know why you had to stop.

Octagonal sign. Red traffic light. Red flashing light. STOP!

Something crosses your life's path . . . interfering with the pace. Graduation was like full speed ahead. Now you are forced to stop. STOP.

Sickness causes a cessation of normal activity. Maybe a stay in the hospital forces a complete halt. No money in your pockets calls for a halt to fulfilling immediate plans or future dreams.

Like being out on that lonely country road, you don't understand why the STOP signs appear. Why must you grind to a halt when everything has been going so great? When you've graduated into something exciting? Why not continue at the same pace or simply slow down a little?

God doesn't always indicate why He sometimes calls us to a complete halt. He has reasons which we have to wrap up in catch-all verses such as Romans 8:28, "We know that in everything God works for good with those who love him, who are called according to his purpose."

His reasoning is somewhat explained in Isaiah 55:8, "For my thoughts are not your thoughts, neither are your ways my ways, says the Lord." He knows where the STOP signs belong. He knows how often we need to cease activities. He even calls us to "be still and know that I am God" (Ps. 46:10).

There's one big area of life in which STOP signs should continually crop up. Yet we often miss them. Sometimes we seem color-blind or our senses are dull. This STOP is defined in Isaiah 1:16, 17, "Cease to do evil, learn to do good."

This is good advice. It's also an absolute necessity if we are to please the One on whose way we are traveling. STOP doing evil. It has no place in the life of the Christian—young or old. It is contrary to God's plan for our lives.

Notice Isaiah adds something after advising us to STOP doing evil. He tells us not to simply stay behind the stop sign. Stop yes, but go on. "Learn to do good." That's like saying go back to school to add a new dimension to one's journey. And in doing good one can go full speed ahead!

YOU APPROACH AN INTERSECTION. It has two lanes going your direction. One veers to the right. A sign on the post reads "Right lane must turn right."

You notice a driver in front of you has decided to go straight ahead. He shifts lanes, almost causing fender wrinkling. Horns blast. You proceed with caution into the right-turn lane. When your opportunity arrives, you obey the sign. Just like they said in drivers' ed. You wanted to go that way anyway, so you obeyed the sign. You did what was expected.

The Christian young person often faces "Right Lane Must Turn Right" signs in life. He is going along life's way in the mainstream. Unnoticed. Most of the time he isn't recognized as being a Christian. He does the same things others do—it's all part of ordinary life. Yet at times everyone around knows his religious convictions. It's a necessity!

In either case, he's on his own. He's in the adult world now. He has to make the decisions which way to turn. If he's in situations where most people know he is a follower of Jesus Christ, they expect him to make certain moves—to turn to the right. They are surprised if he doesn't. Going straight ahead in their wrong way even shocks the onlooker. Besides, such action is a reflection on the Christ one claims to follow.

What does the Christian do in a situation where no one knows his religious connections or convictions? Does he say, Nobody knows me? I can do as I please. My parents can't tell me what to do now! Or does he have an obligation to himself and to his Lord to turn to the right? Such action should be automatic, done out of love to the Savior.

James proclaimed that if you don't turn to the right when it is expected of you, you actually sin. "Whoever knows what is right to do and fails to do right, for him it is sin" (4:17). It's sin no matter who is watching . . . or to whom you are now responsible. This is one thing you never graduate from—responsibility for what you do!

When Peter preached to Cornelius, he said, "Truly I perceive that God shows no partiality, but in every nation any one who fears him and does what is right is acceptable to him" (Acts 10:35). In the same breath he connects fearing (believing in, reverencing) and doing what is right. They can't be separated. One can't claim adherence to God and not practice doing what is defined as right. Unfortunately some Christians have divorced their beliefs from their practices. Some youth have thrown off parental directives.

Turning right when it is expected makes you an adult almost unawares. It also puts challenge into life. It gives you an excellent opportunity to be aligned with the Lord who made you. It tells the world you are one of His representatives. And isn't that a great part of what your faith is all about? Turning to the right is a Christian's privilege.

HAVE YOU EVER DRIVEN down a paved road which has seemingly been repaired by an amateur? Or maybe the road hasn't been repaired in a coon's age. You bounce over potholes or buckled and cracked pavement. It has been this way for several miles. Suddenly you come to another yellow diamond sign. It reads "Rough road ahead."

You laugh. Nothing could be worse than the kidney bouncer you've just traveled. But you're wrong. The road proves the sign wasn't kidding.

Sometimes the state highway department gives you a cheerful addition: "Rough road next 13 miles." You groan, keep an eye on the odometer, and bounce along. Sure pays to trust your shock absorbers to work overtime without a groan. Once in a while you think they've gone on strike . . . or was it the springs? You mumble about the roughness. It won't do your tires any good . . . and they weren't so good to begin with.

Oh, the joy when the thirteen miles are passed. Suddenly you seem to float along on a newly paved section. You're almost ready to write a thank you to the governor . . . or was it a complaint in memory of the bouncing?

Life has many rough roads. If you thought schooling was rough, be prepared. This is another thing you'll never graduate from. In fact, sometimes along the way you'll feel you are on a perpetually rough ride. One problem will pass only to bump onto another. And occasionally you'll get warnings of a rough road for several months. Not too long from now you'll be facing what your parents face—business declines, child rebels, double-crossing friends, sicknesses.

Everyone is tempted to complain about the road he is on. Why do others seem to have it smooth? Why does my way always seem rough? Aren't there any alternate, easier routes to the same destination?

Several Scripture writers understood the values of a rough road. Character is developed much deeper and fuller when one grasps the meaning of rough driving. To rebel at such times when roughness produces physical, emotional, or economic pains is to reveal a shallowness and immaturity in one's inner self.

Let's look at some of the reactions to bumpy roads made by Isaiah, John, the Psalmist, and Job.

"And though the Lord give you the bread of adversity and the water of affliction, yet your teacher will not hide himself any more, but your eyes shall see your teacher. And your ears shall hear a word behind you, saying, 'This is the way, walk in it'" (Isa. 30:20, 21).

I have said this to you, that in me you may have peace. In the world you have tribulation, but be of good cheer, I have overcome the world" (John 16:33).

"Prove me, O Lord, and try me; test my heart and my mind. For thy steadfast love is before my eyes, and I walk in faithfulness to thee" (Ps. 26:2, 3).

"But he knows the way that I take: when he has tried me, I shall come forth as gold" (Job 23:10).

Rough roads have benefits not immediately recognized by the driver. They prepare us for the full enjoyment of God's eternally smooth way. How good to face the rough road ahead knowing the Lord has already passed that way Himself. Then to trust Him over the bumps. That's living!

FOLLOWING A LOADED TRUCK on a two-lane road in hilly country can be exasperating. It's full speed downhill and a slow creep uphill. The closely spaced no-passing zones prohibit safe passing. Besides, the barreling truck can sometimes outdo you downhill.

What a relief to come to a hill with an extra right-hand lane. The sign at the bottom of the hill reads "Slower traffic keep right." You zoom past the slow truck, happy to leave him behind.

Then one day you have your turn. You rent a truck, load it full of your belongings, and head down the road. Or else you help an older sister or brother to move. The road is a two laner in hilly country. You zoom downhill. Most cars can't pass you. But their drivers become exasperated when you begin the slow uphill pace. Then suddenly you come to an extra right lane. The others seem to take considerable pleasure stomping on their accelerators . . . blast out extra exhaust and zoom by. You are left behind at your slower pace.

Life's highways aren't all four laners. Nor are they all on the level. Sometimes a person has a lot of uphill living to do. You've probably already discovered this in school days—specially around test time. And if someone near you seemed to be blocking your rapid pace to your selected goal, it didn't prove wise to become exasperated. Nor did it show much maturity to zoom past them with a superior attitude. Your opportunity to carry another, even bigger, load uphill might be coming sooner than you think.

When times of designated slower pace come to others, give them a sympathetic and patient look. They'll probably make it to the top of the hill all by themselves. So will we when God builds hill climbing into our experience. Those things that force us to slow down will come regardless of how easy the road seems at present . . . or how wise and strong we think we are. Health problems, financial setbacks, indecisions by ourselves or our friends—these can become life's steep hills to climb.

One can discover two ways to climb a hill. First, observe the top of the hill. Second, look at the road only a few feet in front of your vehicle. Both are necessary to successfully get to the top. But undue attention to either point of focus will cause problems.

If you gaze at the top of the hill you might run off the road where you are. If you never estimate how far you must travel to the top but focus your attention just in front of the hood ornament, you might miscalculate what gear you should use. This could cause the engine to overheat and force you to park on an undesirable shoulder.

David expressed it poetically. "I will lift my eyes unto the hills, from whence comes my strength. My strength comes from the Lord" (Ps. 100:1). This same psalmist also practiced the "few feet in front of the vehicle" approach. He declared in Psalm 37:4, "Commit your way unto the Lord, trust also in him, and he will bring it to pass." He sensed there was a top to the hill. There was also a roadway right under the wheels.

While some seem to be zooming by with ease, the correct combination of these attitudes brings the joyous assurance that when God places a "Slower traffic keep right" sign along our roadway, He knows what He is doing. He has put the top of the hill in His plans too. You'll arrive if you do what seems contrary to youthful driving patterns. Keep to the right and go a little slower. You'll be able to zoom plenty soon. Your turn is coming.

YOU'VE BEEN TRAVELING at a leisurely clip down a highway or on a city street. You've been holding your speed at the stated limit. Suddenly a yellow and black diamond sign with red, yellow, and green circles appears. An additional small sign below it reads "Traffic signal ahead." That's all it says. It doesn't tell you what to do. It's an information sign—except for the fact it's placed on a caution color sign, and shape. That's supposed to tell you something!

Some people pay little attention to such signs . . . specially if they can see the green color of the light. Others push it to avoid stopping in case the light changes to yellow.

Rules of the road instruct the driver to exercise caution when seeing such a sign. Caution usually involves lifting the foot from the accelerator, getting prepared to put it on the brake, and even stopping. Watching approaching traffic, as well as that which is stopped on the crossroad, is specially recommended. You got that question word-perfect on your license exam.

As you travel into your life ahead, you're going to discover many situations have "Traffic signal ahead" warnings. Of course, there will always be instant life-changing circumstances about which no one is ever prewarned. But in those cases in which we are prewarned, it's best to pay close attention and react properly.

Often we get prewarning signals or signs. Something within our thinking just doesn't stack up before we have to make a big decision. Friends don't come across as they had promised. We aren't able to get all the information we need to make a good decision. We're short of cash.

If you've graduated to the position of being on your own, you have to pay even closer attention to the signals and signs ahead. Decisions must be made at a near-at-hand junction. You can't be full speed ahead and paying no attention to conditions or competition. Such an attitude could lead to sudden catastrophe. In business it's called bankruptcy—on the highway it's called a big wreck.

For some reason that only God knows, it doesn't seem good for us to be going full speed ahead all the time. That's why He puts those "Traffic signal ahead" warnings along life's roadway. He wants us to pay attention to others. And even the best kind of living includes being brought to a sudden halt to let others go by.

The word *warn* is used twenty-eight times in various forms throughout the Bible. Possibly the best "traffic signal ahead" verses are in Psalm 19:7-22, "The law of the Lord is perfect, reviving the soul . . . the precepts of the Lord are right, rejoicing the heart . . . Moreover by them is thy servant warned; in keeping them there is great reward."

Ezekiel 33:4, 5 talks about people who hear the sound of a trumpet "and did not take warning." They were as bad off as a driver paying no attention to the yellow "Traffic signal ahead" sign. Stupid to say the least!

Paul told the Colossians he proclaimed the message of Christ and was "warning every man and teaching every man in all wisdom, that we may present every man mature in Christ" (1:28).

Even though one might feel he has graduated into a state of freedom, warnings—like "Traffic signal ahead"—still need to be heeded. When one does, even though momentarily stopped or slowed along the way, he can proceed the way God wants him to travel. God puts up such signs for our good. Proceed with caution.

YOU'RE INTERSECTING with a through highway. Below the octagonal stop sign is a particularly significant black and white rectangle. The top sign tells you to stop. The one beneath warns you that cross traffic does not stop. Drivers will probably zip past you at the legal speed. They know you have to wait. You patiently hold your foot on the brake until all is clear.

The "Cross traffic does not stop" sign has been posted for the safety and enjoyment of all drivers involved. Those on the through highway have the right to a nonstop ride—at least at that intersection. That's one of the privileges of highway or through street driving.

Maybe you've had the experience of having a little brother or sister in the back seat ask you what that sign means. You explain. Then he asks, "Why?"

You go into another explanation. But you

give more of the "how" and "what" than the "why." "But why?" he asks again. In an exasperated tone you reply, "That's why!" without giving an explanation.

It doesn't take much living outside the rather protective atmosphere of school days to discover that many situations in life are like this. Other people seem to be cruising along the smooth highway of life. You end up on a bumpy road. Or else you come across signs with the extra reminder that others can keep on going their merry way with little hindrance while you must stop and wait till they pass.

It's easy to ask God "Why" in such instances. Why must we constantly work while others gain quick and easy success? Why must we struggle and struggle financially?

Why must I observe others getting recognition when I have just as many skills as they? Why does my way of life have so many hindrances to easy going? Why does God seem to rub my nose in it all by forcing me to watch others go along leisurely . . . or even at a full-speed clip?

Remember the incident in John 21:20-23. Peter got all uptight about "the disciple whom Jesus loved" (presumably John). He noticed John getting what Peter interpreted to be preferential treatment. He seemed to be at the crossroad reading the "Cross traffic does not stop" sign. Jesus rebuked Peter rather caustically, "If it is my will that he remains until I come, what is that to you?" In other words, "Peter, just pay attention to your own living."

Rather than envy the easy roads of others, we need to do two things. Pay close attention to one's own way. Second, rejoice that God allows others to live free and prosperously. Yes, the cross traffic does not stop. But leaving sign erecting up to the Lord is far better than trying to second-guess why He allowed us to journey down a particular road. It's a sign of maturity that no amount of schooling can guarantee. But it's a sign of maturity you really want others to see in you. Right?

As you exercise such maturity, without noticing it you'll soon discover you'll be a part of the through traffic. In that mature relationship you'll be empathetic toward those who are having the same experience—waiting at a "Cross traffic does not stop" sign to let you speed by.

WE LIVE ON A CORNER. The street in front of our house is a busy street leading into the heart of our city. The street at our side is a dead end.

Dead end has always had some bad connotations. It sounds so final, so abrupt, so unproductive, so uninviting. Maybe that's the reason the city posts a big yellow diamond to tell the public "Dead end."

For those heading down the street of which the dead end is the end, there's ample warning. They simply turn onto the other street. Once in a while a young couple discovers the dead end a convenient place to park. So in they drive. Otherwise people avoid dead ends.

Life has its dead ends—its unproductive, undesirable places. You've probably experienced a few . . . possibly in some class you had. And somehow or other, even though a graduation certificate indicates a certain amount of wisdom as well as study, no person is ever so sharp as to avoid all of life's dead ends.

Wouldn't it be wonderful if all dead ends—those unproductive activities of life—were clearly marked with big warning signs detectable for a considerable distance from all angles? Surely almost every one of us would switch activities. We'd quickly turn another direction . . . unless we deliberately wanted to park with the desire of producing nothing.

Some people turn into the dead end off the busy street. As soon as they notice the sign or the dead ending, they jam on their brakes, reverse gears, back out into the through street, and go straight. Some appear a little sheepish about the incident. Others smile at their mistake and go on. Others burn rubber.

No matter if their mistake makes them smile or growl, we've noticed how quickly they aim at getting on a street that leads somewhere. A dead end isn't a place to stay for any significant amount of time.

Don't you wish you could discover all your dead ends as quickly? Put yourself into a gear and get out and keep in the mainstream of life. Unfortunately, you usually discover you've been going nowhere after you've been in the dead end for a while. Some classes in school were of that nature. Dead end courses. You wondered why you had to take them. You wanted to get into something profitable or interesting as quickly as possible . . . but it took a whole semester or quarter.

The city street department never puts a sign along the through street to point out you might turn into the dead end. You have to face into the dead end to get the warning. That's why it's so easy to observe the frustrations of people who make the wrong turn. They didn't know it was a dead end until the turn was made.

If a person stays in dead ends in life, there's something wrong inside. Surely the Lord allows almost every one of us to occasionally get on unproductive avenues. You can't avoid every one regardless of how enthusiastic you are about making something out of your life.

Once in a while God seems to park us where no traffic disturbs us. In such a case it's a matter of Christ's call to "come away by yourself to a lonely place, and rest awhile" (Mark 6:31). And dead ends can be quite lonely. God allows this so we'll be better equipped to enter the mainstream of life.

Just in case you've gotten comfortable on some dead end, hear these words from Isaiah 55:7: "Let the wicked forsake his way, and the unrighteous man his thoughts, and let him return to the Lord." The Lord is out in the mainstream of life's traffic. He wants you to join Him out where life is lived on a productive basis. A dead end is no place to stay for long!

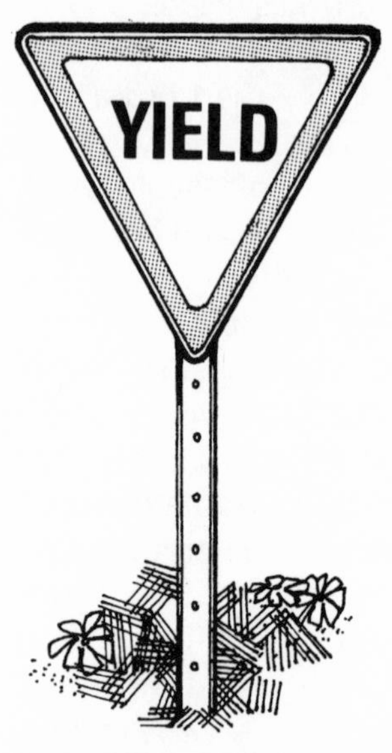

THE RED-EDGED TRIANGLE has become a well-known street and highway sign. It simply means "let the other go before you go." That's difficult for most young bloods. In an every-man-for-himself world, that teaching about defensive driving has a hard time sinking in.

Let's look at a few modifications of this accepted meaning.

Let the other fellow go before you do—specially if pulling in front of him would wrinkle your fenders. But if he's moseying along, take the right-of-way. That's the American way!

It doesn't require too much intelligence to yield to someone who is speeding through an intersection. You'd be crazy not to. Who but the suicidal depressant would invite a crash—and possible death?

Let the other fellow go before you—when you're not in a big hurry. Why rush? You have all the time in the world. Time isn't a factor. You want to enjoy side window scenes as well as the pavement in front of your hood. You can even pride yourself in not being one of those right-of-way grabbers. You want to disprove the reckless youth driver image. It's good for observers to learn this from your driving style as well as from your lips. Of course, example is the best teacher. Maybe your older passengers will be impressed.

Why is it so easy to distort the meaning of the simple yield sign? Doesn't traffic run much more smoothly when each driver obeys . . . and yields? Aren't nerves kept calm and fenders undented when we yield properly? We can calmly move into the traffic pattern once we have obeyed the yield sign.

Life seems to run much more smoothly when we obey yield signs—when we allow others to go before we do. Paul put it even stronger in Romans 12:10 according to the King James version: "In honor preferring one another." This means more than simply yielding. When we give honor to the other person we allow him to go or be first. Then we take the next place . . . or even a little farther back in the line.

Yet it seems so natural to put the modifications into practice instead. We allow others honor as long as we get our own. We slide into our place in the honor line because the other fellow seems to be coming along at too leisurely a pace. We want to get to our destination without delay—often a better job. In order to accomplish our aim (be it conscious or unconscious at the time of an individual act) we have to push ourselves forward. We'd better get into the traffic of life ahead of someone else or we won't make it. Older people seem to think they deserve first pickings. The graduate can wait his turn.

When we misinterpret the timing of life's yield signs or opportunities, we crash into others. That results in resentments, hurt feelings, anger, unfriendliness. And it takes a lot of explaining and rerouting of activities to convince the other person we are really sincere in our yielding.

Have you ever noticed that after you've yielded to some driver, a little farther down the road you might catch up with him or even pass him? That can be true in life also. "In honor preferring one another" might be a little difficult because you haven't been around long enough to be patient. But as you learn to take your turn, God places the yield sign in front of others when you come along. Making yielding a pattern for living will always result in getting you to where God wants you when He wants you! And you don't hinder Him from doing the same for others. It's a great way to live.

YOU'VE BEEN POUNDING THE PAVEMENT. Full speed ahead for five or six hours. Muscles in your legs are tight. It would be a good idea to take time out to rest and relax. You look for the blue sign indicating a rest area. Your anticipation is high when it finally appears and you flash your right signal to pull into the comfortable setting alongside the road.

You stop the engine, open the door, and get out to stretch. Then after a toilet break, you walk around to relax your leg muscles. It's great to stretch. Possibly your family or passengers take advantage of the picnic facilities or drink some of the iron-infested water. The water seems to be 30 percent iron and 8 percent sulphur. You "Wow!" after taking a drink, look around at the various vehicles—from double-dualed heavy duty trucks to pint-sized VWs. Then you head back to your car. Others have similar experiences. Maybe a family dog, who didn't express himself beyond a wagging tail, was the most appreciative of the stop. He discovered a well-visited tree.

Rest areas along the highways help you get to your destination in a more relaxed manner. They indirectly promote safety. That's why you see them everywhere—with facilities tailored for comfort and relaxation.

God knows how much every one of us needs rest areas in life. He even built into our entire physical being a mysterious relaxing process—sleep. Most of us sleep from six to eight hours out of every twenty-four. In fact, every so often you'll pull up to a car in a rest area and see someone taking a snooze. He or she is taking the rest area invitation even more seriously than you.

Now that school days are over you might think about sleeping in in the morning . . . unless you have a job and have to roll out early. Nuts!

But if a person is rested only in body, he can be most miserable. God provides rest for the inner being as well. Call it the soul, your inner being, personality, or whatever. A person needs rest within his mind and soul as well as within his muscles.

Jesus put up a big "rest area" sign when He proclaimed: "Come to me, all who labor and are heavy laden, and I will give you rest" (Matt. 11:28). He knows our inner needs. He knows it is impossible to go full speed ahead for long periods without getting weary, no matter how youthful we might be. He offers inner contentment and satisfaction and cleansing. That truly refreshes. And it's simple to obtain. Simply come to Him—turn from the busyness of life and rest. "Come away by yourselves to a lonely place, and rest awhile'' (Mark 6:31). The Psalmist also suggests we ''rest in the Lord'' (Ps. 37:7).

God set the example early in the world's history. In Genesis 2:3, we read ''And on the seventh day God finished his work which he had done, and he rested on the seventh day from all his work.'' While we don't understand how the Creator of the universe rested or why He needed rest, He set the pace.

The place of rest can be a church building, a quite place in your home, a vacation spot, a special place in a public park, or just a pull-off from the busy traffic of life. Heed God's call to rest. Your entire being needs the refreshment such rest provides. Then you'll be able to get back into the full activities of life. Rest now, work later!

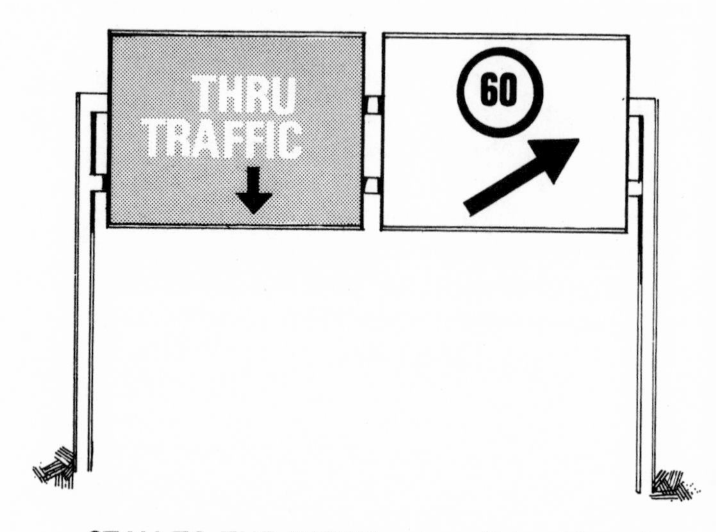

STAY TO THE RIGHT and you'll head into the exit traffic. Through traffic must stay to the left. In fact a big "Thru traffic" sign appears at almost every interchange along interstate highways. The highway commission has even simplified the spelling of the word for quicker identification—THRU.

Remember the first time you drove on an expressway? Remember the exhilaration that set in as you enjoyed the privilege of speed limit acceleration among fast-moving drivers? You passed slower drivers with ease. You relaxed as you viewed the scenery around—specially all the other cars. You talked to those journeying with you. You enjoyed the car's radio music.

But being a part of the thru traffic doesn't allow one to become lackadaisical. You have to watch the road. You must observe the driving habits of fellow drivers. Sometimes they aren't paying proper attention to what they should be doing. Consequently you must remain alert.

The "Thru traffic" sign allows you to anticipate a quicker arrival at your destination. Usually the person traveling in this manner has a definite goal in mind. He knows where he is going.

That's sure an excellent characteristic for all of life—to have a sense of direction . . . to know where you are going . . . to have some goals worthy of your effort. Many graduates can't boast of this. They don't know what they will be doing. Get more schooling? Get a job? Travel? Or just be lazy for awhile!

Have you noticed that the "Thru traffic" sign is always above a straight road? That's one of the advantages of interstate highways. No sharp turns. No "No passing" zones. You can drive down any of the lanes on your side of the median strip. That strip separates you from oncoming cars. You are free at the speed limit to get to your destination.

John the Baptist, in quoting Isaiah 40:3, said, "In the wilderness prepare the way of the Lord, make straight in the desert a highway for our God." He challenged his hearers to get into the "Thru traffic" lanes of the will of God. Notice the emphasis on going a straight way. God's way isn't crooked or devious. Again in Hebrews 12:13, we hear the command, "Make straight paths for your feet." Take the "thru" way.

You've probably heard a couple preachers telling you the same thing. It's old hat by now. Yet it's some of the best advice you'll ever get. It doesn't pay to go the crooked way others sometimes choose just to prove they have freedom or to prove they aren't adolescent anymore. Unknowingly, that's exactly what they prove.

They haven't grown up until they know how to get on the "thru" way.

Traveling God's straight way leads to life abundant. It's the way He planned for those who'll submit to His directions. It's all available by following the guidelines given in His Book, the Bible.

There's another aspect of thru traffic good to consider. Being in the mainstream we have responsibilities to other drivers. As representatives of Jesus Christ we need more than bumper stickers to reveal our identity ("Honk if you love Jesus," etc.). We need to drive in a manner recognized as different. In life, our religion need not be on a placard, bumper sticker, or even on the tip of our tongues. If we're going to represent Jesus in the thru traffic of life, there needs to be something about us that reveals we are God's personal reps.

How long do you stay in the thru lanes? Usually until you reach your turning off ramp. Life is just like that! We are called to live it until God directs us off the exit ramp. Happy motoring down the straight highway at full speed ahead until He so indicates.

Graduation was an entrance ramp. Now you have a long way to travel.

INTERSTATE AND TOLLWAYS have "No hitchhiking" signs at almost every entrance ramp. It's listed with several other No Nos. No vehicles with lugs. No bicycles. No pedestrians. No hitchhiking.

Yet you see them . . . even standing next to the sign! And most of today's hitchhikers are young people. Some haven't even become old enough to graduate from grammar school. There's an equal amount of females and males. Some say there are more females with their thumbs out.

Everyone knows the philosophy behind hitchhiking. The idea is to get a free ride between two points. You simply stand alongside the road, put out your thumb, and hope for someone to stop. The fact so many young people are out doing it indicates it's an inexpensive way to travel. Plenty of drivers stop to give hitchhikers a lift.

Some of the more clever hitchhikers print signs telling motorists where they want to go: Detroit, Chicago, Miami, Los Angeles, Des Moines. Usually they list the larger city toward which they are headed. If they want to go some place near these cities, at least the driver knows approximately where they are headed. He can pick his unknown passenger by city as well as appearance.

The dangers of hitchhiking have been loudly proclaimed. For both the hitchhiker and the driver. The hitchhiker doesn't know who's behind the wheel . . . a drunkard . . . a pervert . . . or just an ordinary person willing to give a needy person a lift. No one knows until you head down the road. Nor does the driver know who's coming aboard. Both hikers and drivers have become victims of crime. Yet there's an increasing number of youths with thumbs up . . . and drivers stopping to give them a lift.

Hitchhiking doesn't take place only on the open road or along city streets. Some adopt it as a way of life. They started quite early . . . even in grammar school. They act as if society owes them a living. Others ought to pay for their existence. Get it free without working for it. Let someone else do the work. Sponge. Let the other guy pay the bill. The world owes me a living.

A lot of people are seemingly getting by on this approach. They rarely put much muscle into producing anything of lasting quality. They work when they must . . . and freeload as often as possible.

You might even have a few friends who fit this pattern. During school days they hitchhiked by copying answers from others during tests. Or they borrowed term papers from last year's students. Or they stole someone's lab project. They never did much that originated within themselves.

And sometimes they hitchhiked a ride from you—specially if you happened to be going their way. Maybe an auto ride. Maybe a completed homework assignment. Maybe a free Coke or whole meal. They managed to get it without shelling out. That's all that counted. And if they succeeded once, they soon became pesty in the practice.

You can hitchhike. Even if there are all kinds of laws against it. Innocently standing beside the road when a police car drives past won't bring arrest in most states. The thumb goes up again when the fuzz are out of sight. You can get away with it . . . get a lot of free rides . . . even get to the place you want to go.

Life allows hitchhikers. No one gets thrown in jail for freeloading. No one is arrested for copying from someone's term paper. No one goes before a judge for sponging a free meal from a friend.

But who really wants the reputation of being a freeloader? There's a deep inner satisfaction from working for everything you accomplish or own. You can look back with pride at your personal accomplishments—even if the method of attainment was rough.

One of the best ways to prove to the adult world that you are maturing is to put your whole heart and soul into everything you do. Make everything you get out of life be in proportion to what you put into it. The world will soon recognize you do it on your own.

There's one place to which every person wants to go . . . but to which no one can hitchhike. You don't arrive there on the merit or efforts of others. You get there only by your own commitment. No person can hitchhike to heaven. You get there by what you personally believe concerning Jesus Christ, not by someone else's faith.

Here are some words from a fellow who wouldn't hitchhike on a long rough road from Jerusalem to Damascus . . . and who met the life-changing Jesus as he walked along. "Never be lacking in zeal, but keep your spiritual fervor, serving the Lord" (Rom. 12:11). Not bad advice for anyone starting out on life's long journey with little money and a lot of latent energy.

PROBABLY EVERY TRAVELER has smiled to himself or joked to other passengers in his car when driving past this sign. On many occasions we've counted the number of men on the job . . . and then the number of men working. The two didn't match. And surely the pavement-fixing job didn't require so many bosses (those standing around).

One teen-ager, when coming past a large orange diamond "Men working" sign, said, "You could have fooled me." There were two flagmen to slow down the traffic. Three others looked like foremen. Two were using air hammers. One fellow was leaning on a stiff-bristled broom. Hardly any of them looked ambitious enough to complete the job. And why did the skinny guys get the air hammer jobs?

One is readily reminded of the ideas in the previous chapter on hitchhiking. These men are freeloaders. So are some workers on road repair crews.

When one comes to a sign which so clearly defines the activity as "men working," he expects that will be what he finds. He is a little disappointed in what goes on—specially right after he has paid his taxes! For *that?*

If you've had a job during school days, you probably came across some who'd meet all the qualifications for being street workers. They seemed to know how much (or how little) work they could get by with and still get a paycheck. The only difference was they weren't stared and wondered at by everyone going by.

Hopefully you've noticed another type of worker, too. It's the fellow who works with the utility company crew after a big storm knocked down trees and tore down electric or telephone lines. He's in an emergency situation . . . but in a sense it's just his job. Yet his attitude is based on the needs around him . . . plus his desire to work. The "Men working" sign tells the truth.

When you go out to get a job, either in the next few weeks or after you've completed additional schooling, you can be one of the above types. Others seeing a "Men working" sign near your life will either say, "You could have fooled me" or else they'll recognize you as a worker. Take your pick.

Even though the freeloaders will loudly proclaim you to be a "company person" or a "pyramid climber" or even some names you'd be embarrassed to repeat, stick with it. Being known as a worker is one of the most satisfying positions to be in. And it's one of the best recommendations when you want to change jobs. Often a new boss is more interested in discovering if you like to work than in knowing what you can do. People are always trainable . . . but rarely can you teach a person to work. Ambition has to be built in by the person himself.

Working is an attitude. It's not based on muscles or brains. You've seen a lot of lazy, muscle-bound lunks. They do only what is required . . . or enough to get by. Or the fellow with the lazy brain. He's a little more difficult to spot. Yet he operates on three mental cylinders out of seven. Could produce a lot more with a little push.

That's what work takes—push. And it doesn't come from the outside. If someone else has to push you, you'll produce only the minimum. But if the push comes from within, your production will be surprising. You'll surprise those around you. You'll surprise your boss. You'll surprise yourself. The greatest thing about all this is the turning of the surprise into satisfaction. Inner satisfaction. You can look at yourself at the end of a day and know you've put your full self into what you did. You've earned the right to relaxation.

Maybe some of your friends have some job recommendations. Some might know of positions with a snap. You won't have to work your head or pants off to make a living at it. Beware of such openings. Look for jobs that force you to stretch either your mind or your muscles . . . or both. Apply with the attitude that you really want to work—not simply to make a name for yourself, but to mature to your fullest potential.

Add the eternal dimension to work. God is interested in what you do. There's really no eternal praise awaiting the freeloader—the slothful. Paul gave one all-inclusive work principle that would be good to adopt as you get your next job: "Whatever your task, work heartily, as serving the Lord and not men" (Col. 3:23). And as Phillips translated it: "Whatever you do, put your whole heart and soul into it." A great principle for anyone who's heading down the work road.

"Men working." A good sign if it's true. But only a point of laughter if it doesn't describe the situation. Surely you never want to have anyone laugh at your performance. And they won't have to if . . . .

THIS SIGN CONTRASTS with a couple others we have discussed. "No U turn." "Right turn must turn right." The one dealt with not turning back. You can't make a U turn in life. Life is always in the now and heads toward the future. It's full speed ahead most of the time. Or when you come to a situation where you can choose between right and wrong, there's really only one wise choice. "Right turn must turn right." That's what's expected of you . . . by both God and men. People depend on your obedience to what is right.

But this "Left turn only" sign is set right in the center of the road. Right in the middle of the traffic. You have to wait either for a green arrow or for traffic to clear before you go.

Actually, turning left is contrary to the flow of the traffic. That's why you have to wait. It's easy to go straight forward. It's also easier to make a right turn. That's why you can even turn right on a red light in most states. You don't interfere with traffic. You don't cause a traffic jam. In fact, you speed up the flow of traffic.

But a left turn is a different action . . . totally different. It can be a big traffic stopper if no particular inside lane has been built for it. That's why street and highway developers have been building that special "Left turn only" lane.

You'll soon discover situations in life where you have to turn left. Kind of go against the traffic. Go your own direction out of the steady flow. Be yourself. Make a decision that others are afraid to make. Even be radical!

Most people like to go along with the crowd. Maintain the status quo. Keep moving in the traffic. Turn to the right because it's easier.

But a left turn is more like going against the traffic. So the world . . . and the church . . . have usually paid special attention to such people. They have put up special places so such people won't disturb the main goings-on too much.

There's recognition that you're around, but please don't disrupt things as they are. Stay in your own "left turn only" lane and let others go by undisturbed. You can do your thing when they have passed.

Maybe you could call making a left turn not going along with the crowd. You've heard that before. Parents are good at telling young people all about that. Be an individual and all that stuff. Be your own person.

Possibly you think you're already that. Yet an analysis of your thinking and activity might reveal something else. You don't make many left turns out of the mainstream of the youth culture. In fact, you're almost a rigid conformist. You wouldn't dare make a left turn. That would tell your friends you were an oddball . . . or not with it.

Yet there comes a time when you have to be brave enough to make a left turn out of the normal pattern. That'll really make you your own person. To even go against your age culture. Unheard of! To do your personal thing regardless of who approves or disapproves.

A young fellow who lived several hundred years before Christ came into this world, made a couple left turns against the traffic of his day. Wow! What consequences. In fact, the rulers of the land put up their own version of "left turn only" lanes and dared anyone to use them. They wanted to trap this young fellow and get his job . . . or even get *him.* Either go down the mainstream or else. . . . What a choice—like making that "left turn only."

What did the young man do? Defied the king's decree. What else? If he hadn't, you never would have read about Daniel in the lions' den. Take a look in the Old Testament book with his name at the top. Read chapter 6. Various district leaders got the king to make a decree that no man should worship any god for thirty days but should bow to the king as god for that time.

When Daniel knew about the document, he immediately got into their "left turn only" lane. He lived dangerously. "He went to his house where he had windows in his upper chamber open toward Jerusalem; and he got down upon his knees three times a day and prayed and gave thanks before his God, as he had done previously" (Dan. 6:10).

Nearly got put to death. You know the story of the lions. Turned left . . . and paid the consequences.

But God stood behind Daniel's bravery. Lions were harmless. And because of his willingness to turn from the mainstream of traffic, the king made him top ruler in the land and even decreed that Daniel's God get full worship by all. What a turnabout . . . or should we say "left turn"?

No matter where you are, God will honor your willingness to be your own person . . . to turn left even when most people want to keep the traffic flowing without interruptions. To follow your peers.

God is looking for modern Daniels. And He'll honor their left turns whenever they feel compelled by a belief that such a turn is life's only course. For some, those "left turn only" signs are the only way to go. Isn't that right, Daniel? And you say those lions are harmless? God had a way of shutting their mouths? He's still the same today? Great!

NOBODY ENJOYS meeting up with this sign. It causes inconveniences. Sometimes you have to go several miles out of your way to arrive at your destination. Almost every detour requires that you reduce your speed. Some detours don't allow any passing because they are only one lane in heavy traffic. Some detours cause traffic jams . . . and delay you when you don't expect it.

Why detours? Widening the road. Fixing potholes. Repaving the surface. Making a new bridge. Straightening out a sharp curve. And sometimes there are temporary detours because of a big accident—an overturned truck on a slippery road, several cars in a pile-up.

No matter what the cause, you are inconvenienced. You are delayed in arriving at the place you want to go. You might be late to an appointment. You might miss the first part of an outdoor movie or sporting event. You might even miss an airplane! You might make a friend wait longer . . . so two people are inconvenienced. But there's nothing you can do about it. You didn't know the detour was there. If you did, you could have planned to take extra time . . . or you could have gone in a different direction.

One sure thing about your life. You haven't graduated into an era of smooth sailing. If anyone has left you with that impression, it's unfortunate. Either he or she hasn't really experienced all of life or else you weren't told the truth. Or maybe the detours weren't fully described. Here are a few you'll come up against sooner or later.

You're planning to purchase a new automobile, have your own well-furnished apartment, entertain friends, take a trip across the country or even to Europe. All sound great . . . and the sooner the better. So you get a job and begin planning how soon each dream will become a reality.

In the meantime you live at home, drive a secondhand heap, and go Dutch treat on entertainments. Your travels are limited to a few neighboring cities. Then what happens? Your car breaks down. It'll take a couple hundred dollars to fix.

Just keeping oneself stalking the ordinary pursuits of life—such as keeping a car in working condition—detours a lot of plans. You have to tap touring savings. It'll require postponing a trip or vacation away from home or getting your new stereo equipment.

At another time you might have sufficient cash. Everything seem to be falling in place. Your plans are well made. Your friends are anxious to be a part of the activities. Specially those who don't have cars dependable enough for the open road. You pack several days early so you won't forget anything. A trip into the mountains with six friends sounds exciting. The camping equipment is all lined up.

Two days before you plan to leave, you come down with a 101° fever. You feel sick all over. The only thing you can think of is a ruined trip. Why did you have to get sick right at this time? Healthy otherwise. Whoever thinks of the flu, or whatever you have, right in the middle of summer? You don't feel detoured—you feel worse than that! Like a train derailment. Why? Why? And how can you react to it?

Or you've been planning to go to a special sports event—stock car championship, football game, tennis playoff, and so on. It wasn't something you exactly *had* to attend. But it would have been enjoyable. Then your parents decide to take a short weekend together. That leaves you to babysit from Friday through Sunday. Your plans are detoured. You'll have to entertain a brattish brother or baby sister. You have to go out of your way to please your parents and put up with your small-fry relatives.

Learning how to react when you suddenly come on a "Detour" sign, whether it's alongside a highway or in any other situation in life, shows how mature or immature you are.

If you begin to talk to yourself—to mumble about why the detour is there—you evidence you haven't grown up. But if you take it in stride, knowing it is aimed at improving conditions for everyone involved—or is something you can't change—you are the victor.

Learning to accept changeable circumstances. Learning to change with the circumstances. Learning how to react to disappointments.

Learning that delays often come unexpectedly. It's all part of becoming a genuine adult person.

Maybe one of the best characteristics to develop is one that doesn't come easy for most energetic youth. That's why the Christian young person has one up on others. It's the fruit of the Spirit within—patience!

Hard to come by in the rush of life. Difficult to practice when things don't go as planned. Almost forgotten in our pressured society. And yet one of the greatest personality traits to demonstrate. Patience. Available because God is within. "The fruit of the Spirit is [along with a lot of other good things] . . . patience" (Gal. 6:23).

Yes. When a big "detour" comes up unexpectedly, you have an inner resource which will help you travel on in peace. No matter what comes, God not only planned it all, but He gives you inner power to come out on top. Detours can become ways by which you get a whole new outlook on life. And there might be a lot of smooth going ahead. Look for it.

INTERSTATES AND EXPRESSWAYS post two speed limits. On top of the sign—the maximum. 55 mph according to national law. Right below it—or on a sign not far down the road—a limit about 10-15 mph less than the maximum. Carefully and clearly marked "Minimum speed."

Why is the sign posted? Why do some people need to be told they have to at least travel at a mimimum speed? Wouldn't everyone want to keep up with the traffic?

No. There are some who would go so slow they'd cause a traffic jam. They like to see the scenery. Notice what's going on from the side windows. Gawk at each possibility.

On streets or highways which list no minimum speed limits, you've gotten stuck behind such drivers. They keep you from going at the legitimate rate. A whole line of cars gets blocked behind them. Nothing you can do—specially if oncoming traffic prohibits you from passing. You wish the slowpoke would turn at the next corner.

Life seems to have a lot of slowpokes—those who don't care how fast (or slow) they move. Those who slow up progress. Those who get in the way when you want to get things done fast. Those who seem to do a minimum (or less) amount of work.

You'll soon discover this type of people. In fact, you probably knew some in school. They wouldn't speed up for anyone. They were content to go slow. It didn't matter whom they were hindering. Or who wanted to rush to something more exciting. They were in slow gear—even though it was high speed to them. Their favorite words: "Don't rush me!" or "Don't get pushy!"

When you get a job, you'll meet some of these minimum speeders. You'd think they were in perpetual second gear with a light foot on the accelerator. Sometimes they work so slow you could almost conclude they would slip into reverse and not know the difference. Maybe they get a bigger paycheck than you. It ain't fair. You'd like to be on an equal-pay-for-equal-work basis.

What does the "Minimum speed" sign really say? Surely it isn't there so anyone can deliberately go slow to impede the progress of others. It's a sort of emergency sign. If it is absolutely necessary to go slower than others, here's how fast you *must* keep going. Otherwise take some side streets.

Occasionally when you're working, you'll have to decrease your speed. When the boss tells you to go at a certain slower clip. When you are on a project which requires special attention to details. When, because of your usual faster clip, you've completed considerable work and can space the remaining work to fill in the required time. Boss's orders again.

But to join the slowpoke makes you no better than he is. He should never be your standard of conduct.

Paul gives some excellent counsel along these lines. He was sort of a full-speed-ahead, keep-up-with-the-traffic sort of fellow. He'd rather die than be a slowpoke. You'd have to watch out he didn't exceed the maximum limit rather than not meet the minimum.

To the Colossians he said, "Whatever you do, work at it with all your heart, as working for the Lord, and not for men" (3:23). When one puts his whole heart into something, he usually doesn't go at the minimum speed.

If you take note of any successful people, you'll soon discover this. They rarely travel at the minimum speed. Let them be your example right off. Even though ambition wasn't a subject in school. And even though some seemed to graduate without it; let it be high on the list of characteristics you will be developing in days to come. That'll keep you moving out into the more goal-conscious, faster traffic. Again, full speed ahead!

WE'VE ALL LISTENED to friends boast about not using seat belts. Some of us have signed petitions against their use. Others have debated the issue of their value in speech classes. But no matter what we say, every car has them. They're installed for our protection.

On the interstates you'll come past brown and white signs with either words or symbols reminding you to buckle up. Experiments have shown these reminders have good effects . . . and help save lives.

In your drivers' ed course you had to buckle up for safety—even when you were traveling at the breakneck speed of 20 mph on city streets. It was part of the course. A law in most states. And your drivers' ed teacher made sure you obeyed this simple order. Whether you believed everything you saw in the class movies on buckling up seat belts, your attention was drawn to their use . . . and the resultant safety they afford. So buckle up!

One good way to remember to be strapped in for safety is to have a little routine to go through before you put your machine into gear. Get in the car. Buckle up. Start the engine. Adjust the mirrors. Put it in gear. Take off. That way buckling up becomes an almost automatic habit. You never start before the belt is secure.

Why all this fuss? First of all, you never know when buckling up will save you from injury or death in case someone causes an accident. You can't buckle up at the moment of impact just before your head hits the windshield. You must be prepared. Emergencies come without warning. It's wise to be prepared.

Now that you've graduated, maybe you think you have all the preparation you need for life. Maybe you've concluded everything will be smooth going from now on. No emergencies. You don't need any special mental or spiritual seat belts to hold you down. They're too constricting. You want freedom . . . regardless of what has happened to friends who have taken laws of life into their own hands. Seat belts are for sissies! Who needs restraints?

Here are a few ideas from some pretty wise fellows. They had a few hard knocks which led them to build some safety factors into their way of living.

Remember the great pop-off Peter? He seemed to run at the lip. Always saying the wrong thing at the right time. He even told Jesus off a couple times. At least he thought he was telling Jesus what was best to do. He matured a little after he got involved in what you'd call "the school of hard knocks"—living out in our big, bad world. After that he could give this advice:

"Gird up your minds" (I Peter 1:13). In our language: "Put a seat belt on your mind. Hold it in place for times of emergency. Be prepared for such exercises."

In Psalm 18:39, we find another value of having a seat belt for life. In addition to couching a little more rigidly behind the wheel, one has a greater grip on what's happening. He's more in charge. So the psalmist said, "For thou didst gird me with strength for the battle." Ah! Another advantage of living by God's rules. He gives strength for living.

Life won't continually come to you as a smooth road without any dangerous cross-traffic situations. There'll be times when you'll have to slam on the brakes. Come to a screeching halt. Almost be wrecked by the greed or carelessness of others. That's when it'll pay to have a strong mind and to find strength through following God's laws. You won't care what beltless friends might say about being sissy. You'll find some real benefits from a controlled mind and a disciplined heart.

Seat belts! Restraints on life? Not if used right. They're all put there for one purpose—your good. Buckle up!

EVERY DRIVER KNOWS what this sign means. He better watch his speedometer. Somewhere up ahead or nearby a policeman in his squad looking at a little meter. The radar equipment sends out an invisible electronic beam which bounces off your car and back to the meter. The meter calculates the speed of the returning radar beam. And you guessed it. The policeman knows exactly how fast you are approaching or going by.

If what the policeman reads on the meter is somewhat higher than the speed listed on the speed limit sign, you're caught. Without excuse, too! All he does is recite what the meter indicates.

A foolproof method for catching anyone going beyond the speed limit. Even if they do it unconsciously. How does the policeman know whether you speed by accident or by deliberate thought? The radar can't read your mind. All the policeman knows is you're going too fast. And you know the results. You only wish he'd turn off those big Mars lights which tell everyone around you've been caught. How embarrassing . . . specially if friends go past!

You never know where the radar man might be. Sometimes he's right out in the open. Sometimes he's just over the crest of a hill. Sometimes he's parked on a side street.

If you are going the legitimate speed or a little less, the radar man won't even move. You are doing what you ought. But if you are going past the stated speed, his roof lights brighten up rather fast.

A lot of quick-footed drivers think a strip of metal or even leather hanging down from the rear axle or bumper will confuse the radar. Don't depend on it. Even these fellows get caught. And you just can't argue against radar.

You'll soon discover, if you haven't already, that God somehow has a radar system going. Specially when you sin. He doesn't usually flash some big lights for everyone to notice every time you sin . . . but He measures your sins. He also lets you know when you have sinned.

Back in the Old Testament, Moses wrote some interesting words. They are like spiritual radar. "Be sure your sin will find you out" (Num. 32:23). That's right. God's radar works on the heart of a person. It tells whether we have sinned or whether we're obeying God's commands.

In Romans 6:23, Paul makes this sobering statement: "The wages of sin is death." There's a penalty to pay once God's radar has revealed we are sinners.

But no one has to stand around gawking when God's radar penetrates our lives to reveal how we've broken His laws. No one can look down on us to make us feel embarrassed. The reason: "All have sinned and fall short of the glory of God" (Rom. 3:23).

Be thankful that God brings your sin to your attention. You really don't want to wait and live a long life as a sinner. And when He arrests your attention it isn't for the purpose of punishing you. He doesn't give out any tickets (at least not until eternity, when men pay the ultimate price for sinning). Rather He stops you so He can offer forgiveness. And like Jesus told one woman He spoke to, "Your sins are forgiven. Go and sin no more."

God wants to offer you that same type of forgiveness. You can take it because it is not offered as a punishment for disobeying the law; it's offered as a free gift. "The free gift of God is eternal life in Christ Jesus our Lord" (Rom. 6:23). That's worth getting stopped for, isn't it?

ONCE IN A WHILE YOU have to slow down. Traveling on a state highway, you come to a town. Speed limits are reduced considerably from highway speeds. Sometimes you suspect the small town has designed special speed traps. Like going 20 mph through town. Incredible, specially after doing 55 for nearly three hours.

But once you get to the edge of town, you get the joyous news. The sign reads "Resume speed." You push it and get on your way. Maybe you mumble about having had to slow down. But you were happy. No uniformed man with Mars lights stopped you.

There's another time you'll run across this "Resume speed" sign. You are out in the country. Suddenly some orange construction signs pop up. The pavement is being repaired. You are urged to slow down. Maybe you have a little jogged detour to follow. You slow down to the recommended speed . . . or at least to some speed near the sign's request. When you come to the end of the construction, you meet the "Resume speed" sign. You're glad . . . and then press the accelerator. Full speed ahead.

This is a rather interesting idea to follow a discussion on minimum speeds. There we were faulting those who deliberately slowed down when they didn't have to . . . or when they should have been going at a faster pace. Now we're saying there's a time when slowing down is the thing to do. What's the difference?

We've noted the slowpoke is slowing down when he shouldn't. In this chapter we're talking about going through deliberately planned slow areas. You'd better slow down—or else! It's a slow-down-and-live proposition. The last one was a speed-up-and-live process. Both are in order at the proper time.

You've gone through some of these deliberately slow spots at school. Tests seem to be the biggest slowing device. Teachers seem to be like policemen waiting to catch you for speeding through their courses. They inject some slow areas that made you study . . . and almost park every other activity at the time.

Or once in a while God seems to put a slow time into your life . . . right when you seemed to be making such good time on life's road. Sickness. A broken arm or leg. A broken down car. Parental plans. Moving to a different state. Big slow areas!

The obvious questions to ask are "Why me, Lord?" "Why did this happen to me?" "Why must I slow down when things seemed to be going so good?"

These questions don't always have easy answers. Often no multiple choices are listed.

The school of life doesn't ask you to check "slow," "medium," "fast." Only one sign pops up—"slow!" You wonder why. And above all, why can't God give an answer? Why is He so silent? Doesn't He know everything about what's going on?

In Romans 8:28-29 we get a partial answer: "We know that in all things God works for the good of those who love him, who have been called according to his purpose. For those God foreknew he also predestined to be conformed to the likeness of his Son." Not a bad purpose for what happens in life. Not a bad way to view things that happen. When you understand that God has a purpose in what happens, you can slow down or speed up rather casually. Resume speed whenever you get a clear indication from the Lord, specially through His Word, the Bible.

UPSETTING THE ECOLOGY. Thanks to the concerns of high school and college youths, to ecologists and naturalists, to conservationists of all kinds—we're slowly beginning to pay attention to our environment. Ecology is a big . . . and needed . . . interest in our world.

Big green signs. Yellow diamonds. Special black and white information signs. Rustic roadway signs. All telling us something about protecting nature around us. Deer crossing. Don't feed the bears. National forest. Wildlife refuge. Picking plants prohibited. No hunting.

Probably one or two required courses in school dealt with ecology. Balance in nature. The effects of pollutants. What happens when city developments crowd into natural areas. Big industrial expansion into undeveloped nature areas. In fact, some of the things you studied probably scared you. Birds becoming extinct.

Fish so polluted you wouldn't dare eat them. Streams so contaminated you can't swim in them. Air so murky it becomes dangerous to breathe. Food treated with insecticides harmful to your health.

Okay. What does that say to today's graduate? Most would like to shake adult shoulders because of industrial contamination of air, water, land. Blame the older generation. But every graduate joins the crowd. He drives a car—exhaust! He uses other chemicals. He uses a spray can on himself . . . on his car. He wants things . . . created in factories that pollute the atmosphere. He wants to be entertained. To enjoy hunting, fishing, picnicing, sports, and so on. All with ecology-disturbing possibilities.

One of the first instructions God gave to Adam in the Book of Genesis dealt with ecology. He told him to "have dominion over the fish of the sea, and over the birds of the air, and over the cattle, and over all the earth, and over every creeping thing that creeps upon the earth. . . . Be fruitful and multiply, and fill the earth and subdue it" (Gen. 1:26, 28). Man was to control nature—to keep it in balance.

Unfortunately, man hasn't obeyed this too well. He has raped so much of nature. Greed and a desire for pleasure have caused this. Rather than keeping nature and our earth's resources in balance, man has destroyed so much of it. He hasn't thought about preservation. His main concern has centered in satisfying personal, present goals.

So there is a big challenge set before you. During your lifetime you can either destroy more of nature or else help bring back a healthy ecological balance.

But it won't be easy. You might have to park

your car and walk. Or shoot at targets instead of birds or animals. Or put up with a few more bugs and mosquitoes instead of squirting bug spray in every direction. You might have to decide to enjoy less now in order to enjoy more later. If it's the other way around, soon you might be left with considerably fewer enjoyments. That's the prospect you've graduated into if our ecology is to be saved or even improved.

Those animal-crossing signs are reminders that we must pay attention to nature. Nature can't take care of itself, specially when man keeps killing it off or polluting it. It dies. And who wants to have a lifeless ecology. The best way—discontinue the slow funeral.

God put the plants and animals in their order throughout the world for an intended purpose. To keep things in balance. To produce food for one another . . . and for us. To enhance man's surroundings.

Keeping it that way has to be more than something to study in textbooks. It's more than something you can leave to other busy adults around you. Why not find some ecology-minded organization into which you can put both brain and muscle energies? Why not start today to do something to restore ecological balances . . . to clean up and build up our natural environment. It's a great challenge . . . a challenge any American youth can devote mind and muscle power to on a continuing basis. Sign up under that big tree where you see the squirrels playing and from which you hear the next bird calls! Then begin to watch carefully—soon you'll see deer crossing where the highway departments have erected the signs. That's a great sight to see.

IF YOU LIKE SHOPPING, you'll enjoy following this sign. That's where the interesting stores are located. That's where you'll find displays of clothing, food, tools, gifts . . . and lots more. The sign indicates an area in your city or any town specially designed for the purchasing of merchandise which you want or are attracted to. It tells you where to find business establishments. And if you have a little money to spend, the business district seems to be much more inviting. So you turn your car in the direction indicated by the "Business district" sign. And once you find a parking spot, enjoyment is ahead.

Life seems to have a never ending number of business districts. Some are fascinating . . . alluring. Some will only allow for window shopping —an empty wallet will see to that! Some will supply necessities—things you absolutely need like soap and deodorant and tooth paste and food. Others will entice you to want things you really don't need.

And some business districts will simply be places where you get involved in traffic congestion that slows you down and hinders you from arriving at a destination early. Yes, that black on white "Business district" sign can either be an enticement to a happy shopping spree or a warning to expect a slowdown in traffic.

Whatever the attitude you have toward business districts, one thing is for sure—that's where much of the action is most of the time. That's where people buy and sell. Clothing. Furniture. Food. Drug store items. You name it. It can be had in most business districts. Happy is the person who knows when to enter a business district and when to avoid one.

The call of the business district is to do business. It ain't a call to pleasure . . . or a call to sports. It's a call to spend what you have. To get involved in business transactions. A call to purchase.

Sooner or later all of us have to go into the business district. Necessity calls us. Curiosity gets the best of us. "Let's go downtown" can be heard in most American homes . . . and probably in most countries of the world. But shopping is a life-gripping American habit.

While some shopping-haters seem to successfully keep away from business districts, necessity will occasionally make a shopper out of even the most reluctant of them. They have to purchase some needed items. And so downtown they travel into the business district.

Just as it is impossible to fully avoid the business district in your hometown, so it is impossible to avoid getting involved in the thick of things wherever you live. God wants you right in the business area of life—where you have to make contact with others, where you have to spend your energy and time to make life what it ought to be for others, where you not only take care of your own necessities but pay attention to supplying the necessities of others around you. There are plenty of business districts where you can get involved with the needs of others.

In a sense, God calls each of us to become the person behind the counter . . . supplying what others need or want. That's exciting. You can be an instrument for the good of others . . . and the glory of God.

"Business district" signs are calls to involvement with other people. Don't look at them as warnings that you'll get slowed up on your pleasurable journey. God's business signs are calls to involvement with others. They are much more than signs to call you to supply personal needs. He wants you busy being a giver as well as a receiver.

Doing business for the Lord is the most exciting way to live. Whenever you get an indicating sign calling you to do some business for Him, be sure to turn His way. Supplying the needs of others can be one of life's most satisfying endeavors. There's business ahead. To that you have been schooled and to it you have been graduated.

MAYBE YOU HOPED YOU COULD get through this book without being told there is a right and a wrong way to go. You wanted to learn that for yourself. Maybe you've told your parents or some other advice-giving adult not to tell you what is right or wrong. You know! Yet adults seem bent on telling you what's right or wrong. So here we go again.

But it isn't only parents who tell you this. And though you might feel you've graduated into full freedom, every so often you're going to come up to something or someone who'll tell you in no uncertain terms exactly what this sign says: "Wrong way, do not enter."

Unfortunately, you're like all other people in our society. You don't know everything. And the further you get away from your graduation day, the more you'll realize this. Somehow a person seems to get dumber as he grows older.

Or at least he realizes he doesn't know as much as he thought he knew earlier.

One of the most difficult things you'll face as you travel through life is the matter of always making right decisions. You'll have to select friends. Change jobs. Select a marriage partner. Decide where you'll live. What additional schooling you'll get. What automobile you'll own. Where you'll go on a vacation. What type of charities you'll support with your money, time, and talents.

Decisions. Decisions. Decisions! And it's easy to make wrong ones . . . specially if you haven't had any previous experiences to guide you. Or if you don't like to be told. Or if your friends decide to do things you don't quite approve.

In so many situations there's no one to really help you out. No mother's voice. No father's cautioning. No teacher to give suggestions. You're on your own. And a lot of voices would beckon you to turn their way. You have to make the right decisions . . . all by yourself!

That's why when something or someone indicates to you there is a wrong way as well as a right way, don't resent it. Give it as careful consideration as you give to one of those big red "Wrong way" signs on an interstate.

Maybe you've read about someone who hasn't paid any attention to the "Wrong way" signs on an expressway. The person kept going against traffic. Now he's occupying a small lot in the local cemetery. Maybe he severely injured some innocent person along the way. What a tragedy . . . he had his way—the wrong way!

It's true in many aspects of life. There's an obvious wrong way. There's also an obvious right way. The road we take depends entirely on the decisions we make. We can blame only ourselves if we end in tragedy through deliberately wrong decisions. And it ain't worth it just to prove we can decide against what someone advised us.

It's great to have signs along the way to help us make good decisions. And though you have to make the final leap all by yourself, be thankful for indications which help. That's a mark you are maturing!

The Psalmist made it quite clear in the first sentence of his book. He put up some clearly printed "wrong way" signs long before superhighways blossomed. He said: Happy is the man who doesn't take his advice from wicked people, and decides not to go along with the "wrong way" crowd.

It's interesting. Wherever you find a "Wrong way" sign on a highway, there's a right way—usually by turning to the left or right. It's not difficult to make the proper decision. And only the foolish person goes the wrong way.

There's also a way in the Christian life to help you make the right decisions. It isn't based on listening to a mother, father, older brother or sister, or teacher. You'll find it in Proverbs 3:5, 6: "Trust in the Lord with all your heart and lean not to your own understanding. In all your ways acknowledge him and he shall direct your path." Can't go the "wrong way" if you follow that right way advice. And a lot of people who do, have found it's an exciting way to live.

There's so much more excitement, adventure, and satisfaction in going the right way. So when someone or something comes your way indicating something's wrong ahead, rejoice. You'll find the right way a much better way to live. Try it, you'll like it.

EVERY BOOK has a final chapter. So does life. Some books come to an abrupt close. So do some lives. Every book has its final words. So does every life.

It doesn't take too much wisdom to conclude that this is the final chapter. But what about your life? Are you already in its final pages? But more significantly, are you prepared for the exit if it should come suddenly?

You've been traveling over some interesting roads through this book. You've come across some interesting and challenging signs . . . some interesting concepts by which to live. Some of the signs called you to pay particular attention to the road: to slow up or speed up . . . to turn or go straight . . . to stop or start . . . to go left or right . . . to detour or join the thru traffic. Hopefully you've learned some concepts which will make life more exciting and eternal in quality.

Hopefully this has been a useful graduate's guide to happy living. You probably want to read it again, starting with that big "One way" sign and refreshing your mind with these travel guidelines to happy living. It'll make life ahead more meaningful.

But now you face it . . . just like coming off an interstate or expressway. The sign says "Exit." That means this is the getting-off place. You can't back up. Big red signs seem to scream "Wrong way." You have only one way to go—"Exit."

Sooner or later you're going to face life's "exit" sign. It might not be as soon as you close the cover of this book. It might not be after you read your next book . . . or drive your next one hundred miles . . . or live your next year . . . or even in the next decade.

You have no control over when God shunts you off onto His "exit" ramp. He and He alone has determined when you get off this life and exit into the life to come. You can't avoid the day or the hour. When God says "exit" to your soul, that's the moment of truth.

It might come slowly . . . when you slowly creep toward death's "exit" sign via a lingering illness or accident-produced agony. It might come as abruptly as an auto smack-dabbing into an immovable telephone pole or big tree. The timing is in God's determining power.

But we don't want to end on a morbid note. For the person who has placed his trust and confidence in Jesus Christ, entering heaven isn't the end of exciting living—it's a beginning of something far better than any highway a man can travel on the earth. Jesus said, "In my Father's house are many dwelling places . . . I go and prepare a place for you . . . and if I go and prepare a place for you, I will come again and receive you to myself so where I am you may also be" (John 14:1-3). That's exciting. Heaven's beautiful streets aren't anything like the weather-beaten ones on which you have been chugging along.

No fear to exit. That's right. You don't have to fear leaving this life. You simply have to be prepared. And that preparation isn't as complicated as trying to read some of the interstate or highway signs around our big cities. The way is clearly marked. Jesus said, "I am the way." The method is simple: "Believe on the Lord Jesus Christ and you will be saved" (Acts 16:31).

Those who have made the proper preparation to exit don't sit around worrying about it. They live life with zest because they know there's another zestful life awaiting them beyond. They live life with purpose—purpose established by the planner of time and eternity, the God of the universe whom they know on a person-to-person basis through a vital linkage to Jesus Christ. They don't get hung up on too many dead ends or side roads. Life is productive and filled with meaning. Jesus Christ is out in front of them, setting the pace for all of this life and the life to come. As the writer of Hebrews proclaimed, "They have fixed their eyes upon Jesus, the pioneer and forerunner of their faith" (12:2).

You can live in the same manner. And if you've integrated this book's guidelines for happy living into your thinking, the "exit" sign won't scare you one bit. You are already prepared to meet your God.

Happy living . . . according to the concepts and commands of Jesus Christ . . . prepares anyone for happy dying. Be prepared.

And be prepared for a lot more happy living

along the highways and streets of your life. People around you need to see expressions of joy coming from your life . . . and to experience some of these guidelines for happiness brushing off on them because of your living.

Aren't you glad you graduated . . . into a full life here and forever!